Lift

Harry Man

LIFT

ISBN – 13: 978 - 1 - 904551 - 99 - 7

A CIP record for this title is available from the British Library.

Published by tall-lighthouse press.

ACKNOWLEDGEMENTS

Thanks to the editors of the following publications in which some of these poems have appeared previously: *New Welsh Review*, *Poems in the Waiting Room*, *Popshot Magazine*, *And Other Poems*, *Fuselit*, *Coin Opera 2: Dr. Fulminare's Revenge*, *Elbow Room*, *Astronaut*, *ditch*, *Eyewear Poetry Focus*, *Poetry Digest*, *The Morning Star*, PEN International's *Made Up Words* Anthology and *Poems in Which*. 'Lost Ordinance' received third prize in the Cardiff International Poetry Competition and 'telesue' achieved second place in the 2013 PEN International Made Up Words Competition.

Thanks to Gareth Lewis, Tim Liardet, Carrie Etter, Annie McGann, Nikita Lalwani, Ros Wynne-Jones, Philippa Milnes-Smith, Karen McCarthy Woolf, Matt Bryden, Patrick Early, Simon Barraclough, Loki Hamilton-Wright, Todd Swift's Maida Vale workshop group, Malika's Kitchen, Heidi Williamson, Stephen Knight, Alex Anstey, Kirsten Irving, Gwen Davies, Chrissy Williams, Edward Brooke-Hitching, Literature Wales, Arvon, Will & Sarah, my friends and family and those I have missed, and, above all to Jennifer Essex.

For Donny, Donny, Donny, F & J, because a promise is a promise.

CONTENTS

More than anything else the sensation is one of perfect peace mingled with an excitement that strains every nerve to the utmost, if you can conceive of such a combination.

Wilbur Wright

The Last Words of a Lovesick Time Machine Pilot

And would you ever know if I had
snatched the keys from under the mat,
and unlocked the nucleus of our parents' old Astra
with its quarks of petrol and spent Silk Cut packs

and taken my younger self for a spin
past the shutters lit blue from within –
the freezer light of Kennedy's fishmonger's
not Frankenstein's lab after all – sorry,

and told you, Donny, this one's important:
do what you were going to do and ask Susie Whitlow
on a date— yes, like last Wednesday when you tried
at Latchmere slides, feeling doubly sick from the height

and your nerves on the diving board ladder –
I shouldn't remind you – but in ten years' time,
over a bottle of wine, she'll tell you she has
a new boyfriend, whose name, you joke, sounds

like a make of saucepan, which isn't so funny
for you, so much as a blow but sometimes
a little hurt is worth a heartful – like baking
with Dad while nursing a broken foot

from that casserole dish you failed to lift,
and don't leave for Dover without matches,
and put a couple more quid on Little Polveir
at the Grand National this year, but still

slip the winnings into the lining of Mum's Dorla purse
like you were planning and, when pulling up home again,
I say, this is my last visit, I'm restoring the timeline,
so you should go and tip-toe inside and pause for a beat

on the third stair, and when the past's within walking distance
try not to startle all three of your selves on the landing
or you'll wake everyone up and we won't make it,
and Mum wants answers and Dad gets sick

and don't recall our talk to anyone,
over time it will blur, and merge;
let's call me the best of a good conscience
and say these things, and only these things

meaning when you test the Burnell core in Culham
after the press conference, you keep curious,
stride into the temporal displacement unit,
feeling in your atoms you might never know?

telesue

*n. one of the hundreds of people who look like Sue from far away,
but are in fact strangers.*

Cottoning on too late, the Herne Hill train sparking slow
away into the sleet, that you are not you, but a telesue
coming in from the wings of the platform to play a cameo,
and I remember the background buzz of a fancy dress shop
as past tense as your maiden name, the pop and slup
of trying on fancy dress masks of cow heads, stormtroopers
and elven faces – shrieks as the elastics stripped our hair, stooped
almost kissing as I freed you and you freed me, and lost touch.
Now you're just a Yahoo email address and a year, a smudge
of a photo from that Halloween party, you and your Carlsberg
leaning focusless into the frame, and here in the sleet the telesue
lips a favourite-coloured scarf against the wind, but Sue, real Sue
there are days I don't believe in doubles or daydreams,
when you're behind every windscreen of every car coming
    the other way.

The Only Woman to Have Walked on the Moon

This soft side of the knuckle of my hand, wrinkled,
calved, a planetoid, bone dust, a sliver of a sister,
adventuring to the nearest heavenly body and this?
So close and hot, men must go mad.

Don't you remember I was never here?

The Discovery

Flight of Saturn V SA-511
Apollo 16, CM Callsign Orion, LM Callsign Casper
Command Pilot: John W. Young,
Command Module Pilot: Thomas K. Mattingly II,
Lunar Module Pilot: Charles M. Duke Jr
16th April 1972

A Saturn V sheds her heavy feathers
in the smoke, a rising asterisk of light,
the tank, pencil-slim, gimbals
twisting through the portal
between us and the airless shallows
of our immediate orbit.

The second stage too falls away
and for a split second
the pilots are blinded
by a vapour hotter than lightning
only to open their eyes
in the uninterrupted night.

It is so very still up there
mission control becomes wind,
your own hands the horizon
the difference between day and night
in the humming of lights
and a sense of home
nearer than a fireproof flight plan
nearer than freeze-dried blueberries
the sound of your own heart
in the night-time
a picture in crayon
from your son
which says 'Daddy'
with the Moon
drawn in purple
and an arrow
for guidance.

Sheep Get Inquisitive after a Meteor Strike, Stanbury Moor

Some spacefall has shot
burnt, skiddering into the fallow
sheep field on Stanbury Moor.

We did not see the meteor
sear down into the clover
overnight but its flight path
was caught by a local man
on the dangling negatives
in his darkroom –
a white tick on a dusty blackboard.

In the morning, sheep mill around
the crater edge, stumble up out of it
and dodder away as we tread closer,
heads bobbing, chewing
with the expression of someone who thinks
they can hear the telephone.

With a first plunge into the ground
the grass rips – we want this one for eBay –
afraid, inquisitive, stock still,
the sheep look at us
like fallen pieces
of the Moon, fallen.

Lost Ordinance, Sussex, 1943
for Patrick Early

Where the light retreats to blackness around the 14th
hole, there is a tank trap. That strip of ochre snow is

an illusion. That hairline of meltwater along the tunnel
underneath smells of burnt pitch, as if a stray shell

struck the skull of the land, and it bleeds, starless,
motherless. Old snow creaks on the roof, like the spirit

of my father on the landing or at the head of the kitchen
gathering the patience to glue our lilac dinner plates back

together. And outside is a sea. I'll say it again. Outside
is a sea where the contingent silence is broken by blue and red

timid shadow fish, smelling like, sounding like, pretending to be
— foxes. The sound on the track of alien scamper but turn

and there is nothing but empty lane, hedgerow... out of eye shot
the muffled barks of sheep. We walk further, further into the street-lit

alders, coppices and their snow-stranded outlines flensed
of their leaves, intermingled with the field's fencing. I write

letters in my mind to where my father is stationed in Rawalpindi
as yesterday I found something in the frost, copper-green

and not a bracelet – we have found Roman remains before –
but a watch, my father's, never worn and too big

for me: a present thrown in anger the night before
he left for the war. I cup its dial in my fingers

and through the condensation I can see still glowing;
the radium hands seized at the stroke of midnight.

My Older Brother Is a Self-Contained Binary Star System

The days burnt down to medlar branches
the colour of hands, no longer killing time
thrashing nettles in the derelict orchard,

you and me, my brother, finishing
your stories of detective racers, and werewolf thieves,
the interdimensional girls, the mirror-maker

turned vampire hunter, the scrieving cedars
winking across our languages, ready to type,
swapping input like it was, one idea between two

in the parallaxing flash of binary stars.
Helixes in isolation, growing lank
into old futures, as black holes eat slow matter.

Of a day you named a Hawk T-1 by sound alone
in the morning rays, the plane slipping
the knot of the Worcestershire clouds,

crackling into the chorus of crow squawks,
the weathervane, weak in the wind,
the stopwatch tick of the electric fence.

Another noon, the disused chicken hutch
on fire as if crashed into the planet
with you, its surviving pilot,

strutting away from the blast,
the secret of your x-wing origins
charred out of all recognition.

And now I often mean to phone and say
how at night, those stories you wrote still shine
around my head like heat, like light rays,

like radio waves, like radiation –
how to put it, off every surface
moon-bright echoes, electric.

J. Jonah Jameson

These two-bit hoods don't know he's the enemy still.
Just like their parents, there's no law left but libel.
Get a picture of Spider-Man close enough to smell
his breath on the lens – that's something to sell.
Now's not the time to be throwing in the towel,
or coming up with cracker-jack excuses, hell,
if the dust doesn't do you in, the winters will.
If you ask me, nuclear war's too good for us all.
Throw another in my Daily Bugle mug, be a doll.

In / different voices

Can I just ask / what little / conviction / we have / theft all the time
We can't force / terrorism / in the home / out and about
chances are / or if / They come back / It sounds a perfectly normal
Stupid question / motor vehicle / Do you know what your name is?
As it's assault, just us two / for me please / serious criminal / service
  "TOTAL POLICING" / all that will do / fracture / across the sternum
paperwork matches the description / such / for that individual
arresting / bicycle lights / eschews / the property / inadmissible
be able / To aid / not them, to you right / Say we / offending
persons unknown / When you can / if they come back / in court
we might well say / witness / neighbourhood / If they come forward
despite previous / and that line / goes to court / They go back
It's called stop 'n' search / Thanks for coming in / the profile
not that we think you will fit / commit / the system / allows you
victim / on the pavement so / Fine / premises outside / London
so I am issuing you a ticket / goods we can't / in a month
or so / out of our hands / violate / have out of our control /
out of an impossible / date of birth / on the form / prosecution / free
counselling is available / if you just ask / you can just ask / Shall I,
  shan't I? Shan't I.

Ultrasound

The white artery of your spine
hovers beneath a butterfly's ghost;

wings budding into flight
twice a second, heartbeat by heartbeat.

The isthmus of your foot kicks in the fluid –
the pressure of the sensor is ticklish.

With the end of his biro the doctor
circles your magnified hand gloved in light

and this shimmer, this afterthought of air
in the trees, is the breath of your mother.

Night-blind you will fumble back
to its anthem through the clicks

of your hardening head.
This song, secret as a light switch,

is how your breathing will be.
The warmth of my wrist on your belly;

your pulse and mine in time –
the first of your strengths is to be loved.

Troubleshooting

I have scanned the headlines a hundred times,
and know the perfect way to poach an egg.

My theatrically posed electrical guts
are on display through the roof of my head.

Here my hot parts are highly-prized
by the brave or the certified.

My outpourings are the stuff of office legend
and the game is up, it was me all along –

I swallowed the fiscal year final accounts
and the list of fourth floor first aiders to avoid capture.

I've lengthened the lives of your lost pets
and your permits, your pencilled catalogue pages

your round robin jokes and cautionary notes
the unflattering discs of your buttocks.

But I can't be the hero forever, I get old
and spill food all over myself,

I drink too much, or overexpose,
or become idle in the middle of instruction.

During operations I need a bypass
or risk losing your history forever.

And acting as though nothing has happened
isn't acting anymore, it is how it is
on the tip.

Nightingale is

In practice this nightingale's words swerve, herded into home video
air-stuffled foreground wall sound, the wind that wears at altitude
the aural cavities of avian hearing in the peace from the birch
where wash is a verb of weatherfront heard while circling
the circuit of hand-me-down hunting grounds, microscoping
the Medway-soaked plantain for what itches in the ultraviolet,
signals aeronautic, arcs synaptic across the hindbrain, midbrain,
forebrain, hover-held, a fulgurite voice-print following-fit phrase
memorised in the buffered bee-mind reckoning the rote intones
the thatch calyx of nest and the skull-vaulted song in air sacs
stacks the socketing of gases that surge-electric, sublate,
regulated by the lungs, the heart, the stomach, the stomach,
heart and lungs, the carrier wave of pulse is gyroscopic
through curves, curves of the skin-thick crown coast-magnetic,
less dead cert, but surfs a feeling for North, Norfolk, Shaker's Wood,
next crests hemispheres, never blackening out, dips to pitch, downs
the tent of its wings, falls with the grain of the wind, a skiff skirting
the transparent cerebella of high canopies, weighing sail-search
with why, whichever perch works to see what kill comes
if it comes to kill first and shudders bursts of nerved stuttering,
the head saccading for the sake of the eye, the sinuses hum
in syrinx territory calls, chiaroscuro, resonant, stridulating
lift ululatations, Senegambian, the wind changes —
you hear it; the nightingale, a female singing in nervous laughter,
a musical birthday card addressed to the dead,
a holiday-maker's car alarm – loud and long and penetrating
and worrying between wanting attention and warning,
breaking off into an uneasy peace.

Earth

Born on 22nd April 454 billion BC **You** and **Gravity** are now friends

Your hometown in **Spiral Arm, Milky Way** is 'Solar System' 0 like this

The Moon has indicated that you are brothers Confirm? Accept? Block?

Hi EARTH I would like to add you to my professional network

Fossil Record has indicated that you worked at 'Multi Cellular Life'

Archaea and **Eucaryota** shared a link on your timeline

Bacteria and **Eucaryota** shared a link on your timeline

Vertebrate Animals suggested adding **Primitive Fish** to your list of friends

Today is **Ozone Layer**'s birthday. **UV Radiation** 'Ozone - get a life'

Vendian Supercontinent commented on your **status** 'Great atmosphere' Like?

You have successfully joined 'Cratons and Vendian Supercontinent' network

Ozone Layer invited you to an event 'Party on the surface, UV is BLOCKED!'

Unknown invited you to the event 'The Ordovician–Silurian Mass Extinction' Block

requests from this application? Activity from **Unknown** will not appear in your timeline

Eurasia, Antarctica, India and **North America** recently joined **Pangaea** in your network

Early Mammals, Reptiles, Seeds and 700 million others are now your friends

You have successfully changed your cover picture to 'OneBigGreenblob.jpg' Like?

Sponsored **Devonian Period** likes 'Great Dying & Adaptive Radiation on the Tree of Life'

You are attending 'Great Dying & Adaptive Radiation on the Tree of Life'

Remaining Insects read an article on the Daily Mail 'Primitive Mammals to Block Access to as Many Deceased Permian-Triassic era Facebook Profiles as They Like'

Archosaurs and **Late Permian Period** changed 'In a relationship' on their timelines to 'It's complicated' **You** and **Severe Volcanism** are now friends

Sunlight 'Is Severe Volcanism blocking me? FFS This is a *social* network!'

Hi EARTH I would like to add you to my professional network

Shrew-like Skeletons has indicated you worked at 'Slow Recovery of Mammalian Life'

You and **The First Birds** are now friends **You** and **Stegosaurus** are now friends

Vast Swamps and **Prehistoric Forests** joined 'I Secretly Want Earth to Be a Sludgy Wood Block'

New message from **Dinosaurs** 150 million years ago – *We RULE ur time lein*

Therapsida maybe attending 'Evolving into Early Hominids' in 100 million years - Like?

Gondwana went from being 'in a relationship' to 'single' near **Iapteus Ocean** 0 like this

Microraptors, Hadrosaurs, Flowering Plants and **Massive Asteroid** joined the network

'Goodness Cretaceous Great Ball of Fire' **Massive Asteroid** poked you on your timeline

Marsupials commented on their own status 'So long 75% of my friends FML'

Arboreal Primates has a new role at 'Becoming Homo Habilis: Off the Starting Blocks'

People You May Know: See **All Neanderthals. The Recent Ice Age** is a mutual friend

Humans like Life. **Humans** and **Global Warming** are now connected.

Sunlight Block this person? Report this? 'SETI' Join networking group?

Check out your timeline. What's on your mind? **Earth** more friends are waiting.

Lines Derived from Minecraft Player Queries

Have you ever spawned like this,
clouds passing through your building
and a blocky dog that will not die
and your wheat disappearing?

Today I checked out the far lands.
What is the best use for gold? Apples?
What do you think the future will be like?
The slow pigs, and 1.6 horses.

Will the air be a fluid like lava?
Will the best trap for a diamond
still be lagging after a while,
or a sweet new skin made just for me?

My skeleton is too fast.
There are so many invisible monsters after death.
I am sick of searching for saddles.
I have a question for you guys,
how rare are villages?

Re-entry of the First American in Space
Flight of Mercury-Redstone 3, Callsign Freedom 7
Command Pilot: Alan B. Shepherd Jr
May 5th 1961

The poets were wrong:
the ocean is not unkillable,
the snow is not eternal.

The Earth turns in the depths
like a cat's eye limned
by a distant headlight.

Then there's this ionized,
candescent, compression of air,
a husk of oxygen and nitrogen.

The view from inside a marshmallow
in a camp fire, all blue and hot,
fizzing into plasma, circumzenithal.

Through the plumes,
black horizons, perfectly skyless
spinning above the afternoon,

glittering pack-ice clouds, below
or above these glass deltas of ocean
releaseless, frozen sleek,

at 17,000 miles per hour, tilting away
and back into the viewport,
the altimeter turning anti-clockwise

and your face pinches itself,
you reach against gravity for the drogue
handle, twisting it and a noise

like the crump of a burst tyre
behind your head, in the crosshairs
the jellyfish red and whites

of the main capsule parachute...
lurching against the straps.
Splashdown with no smell of salt

but foam – how it is, polystyrene
and car seats, and your own breath
in the helmet, with a tap-water plitter

that could be the heat shield, your ears
adjusting, or a ruptured seal,
the panel shows cabin pressure

is green. Zoopraxiascopic shadows—
Is it?
It is, helicopter blades, shuttering.

Over the clanks of the Atlantic
naming the sound of home,
"Thank you very much, it's a beautiful day."

Object

(2013)

Text on canvas of found materials
Dimensions 198mm x 130mm (approximate, set by viewer)

Scattered, the words represent forms in their own right and are also significant in their cumulative effect. Between them is space; airy, invisible and blank. This is where the artist is drawing on the influence of 12th century Chinese Zen contemplation, encouraging the viewer to consider his or her own essential nature. According to Zen practices the exclusion of all other thoughts is the only method of achieving pure enlightenment. From the perspective of one word to the next, the viewer can see how none of the words in the text are positioned such that they overlap. This seems to be intentional and is consistent with the artist's other works. This choice is inviting the viewer in. Through an implicit absence of anything to draw their focus, the viewer is encouraged to observe what object emerges, to consider their object and how it is positioned and moves, how it tastes, to listen for any emissions of sound, to sense its individual scent, the texture of it along the palm and the object's heat or coolness. No other viewer of this text either now, in the past, or in the future is imagining the same object. This object is not the work of the artist, it is made from the viewer's essential nature. In this way it is very beautiful and also fragile. The experience itself is not enlightenment because the viewer continues to read the text, but what the viewer is picturing is a trace of it, like when awakening – that first momentary, glowing imprint of light.

Hiromi Miyake
Japanese 56kg International Women's Weightlifting Silver Medallist

The audience at the front; dark white bread in an oven,
each of them expressions as uncompressed as lakes.
Snatch, and nostrils of Wang Mingjuan, trembled, flaring,
pleased and quiet like a mirror, a muscle, a whistle string.
Arrow root lifting-powder poltergeisting about the place.
Mingjuan was a slow motion cat leap into red towels—
happy to be here, happy to compete, happening,
Hiromi Miyake, Hiromi Miyake — not City, Red Army,
The just so so beautiful tonight ArcelorMittal Orbit,
"but works in a bank part time to fund her appetite
for lifting weights..."
the bar is seven reds, retinas, clean, high over heads
of state.

Space suit

Dusk at 121 degrees
          centigrade
              in the crosshairs
of the high definition chest camera,
pixels of an imagined Sheffield.

     Exposed to space
your lungs would freeze,
you'd get the bends.

Orbit's like being asleep in the backseat
   and woken on the crest of a hill
the air crash feeling
      with no resistance,
         or a skyscraper

lift dropping flights
   through a lightlessness.

        Darkness so thick
you could scoop it,
       like shoe polish;
the Pacific,
blank, black, except these arachnid,

   skeletal flashes
of storms,
    there are no furred dots,
not like leaving the bed
      to check

the deadlocks,
     the outline of a human-shaped
clothes horse
behind you.

   The Invisible Man reaching
toward the bolts
         not hearing, not seeing,
   the rub of your own fingers.

                    There is a view
of each star's light
                    the speed of light will let you see;

ancient, utterly sharp,
                    more photograph than real,

not twinkling like airliners
                    in the gas.

Prior to our arrival,
the texture of the Moon's surface
                    was a complete unknown

and spacesuits
                    had to cope with micro-meteorites,
dust fields of unknown depths;

                    the weight
of the backpack
        when running

over even terrain or at elevations.
            If he should topple,
would the wearer be able to rise
        unaided?
The almost hilarious tragedy
            that never was the televised yellow
mylar foil of the Lunar Module
        sinking
                    into a lake of Hadean sand.

Beyond rescue,
                    our planet
nutates in the blackness
        with the nod of a compliant child
                        in and out of the glare
of a star 1.3 million times the size of the Earth.
                Behind the faceplate
                    we who orbit.

The Last Words of a Lovesick Time Machine Pilot

Russian cosmonaut Sergei Krikalev has travelled 0.02 seconds into the future.

The Only Woman to Have Walked on the Moon

Chang'e is a Chinese goddess who, it is said, has been living on the Moon for 4,000 years, supposedly with a jade rabbit for company. The story goes that she was banished to our moon because she stole a pill of immortality from her husband.

In the Apollo 11 flight transcripts, Edwin "Buzz" Aldrin comments, "Okay. We'll keep a close eye out for the bunny girl."

In December 2013, the Chinese probe Chang'e 3, carrying a lunar rover, beamed live pictures from the lunar surface back to Earth.

My Older Brother Is a Self-Contained Binary Star System

Stellar parallax is a method of determining the distance of stars from our planet,

This was initially achieved by measuring the shift of stars when the Earth was at either side of its orbit around the Sun and triangulating the position relative to stationary objects. This type of measurement proved accurate to a distance of 100 trillion kilometres.

This method was improved upon by Henrietta Swan Leavitt, an American astronomer, who worked as a human 'computer' in the Harvard College Observatory at the turn of the 20th century. As she was a woman, she was not allowed access to a telescope. Using 299 photographic plates from thirteen telescopes and looking at Cepheids (a class of very luminous variable stars), she was able to determine the distances between objects far further out in space than was considered possible at the time.

Many years later, as a direct result of her ground-breaking discovery, the astronomer Edwin Hubble was able to establish that the universe in which we live is expanding. Hubble often said that Henrietta Leavitt deserved a Nobel prize for her work. An attempt was made by Swedish mathematician Gösta Mittag-Leffler to nominate Leavitt in 1924, three years after her death.

Nightingale is

Between 1995 and 2009, the British Nightingale population decreased by 57%. At the current rate of decline, within 15 years of the publication of this pamphlet the British Nightingale will be extinct. For information about how you can help save the species visit the British Trust for Ornithology's website at www.bto.org